The Great Spaghetti Suit

Alan MacDonald

Illustrated by Pat McCarthy

OXFORD
UNIVERSITY PRESS

1

'Come quickly,' said Mum. 'You'll never guess who's in the shop!'

I ran into the shop with Rolo at my heels. Rolo is my dog. Where I go Rolo goes too.

In the shop was a very large man. He wore a large hat and a coat over his shoulders. Rings of smoke puffed from his fat cigar.

'Who is it?' I whispered to Mum.

'Don't you know? It's Bernard Bellow, the famous singer. He has a voice like an angel. I've got all his CDs.'

'What does he want?' I asked.

'He wants to buy a suit.'

Our shop is called 'Sue's Suits'.
Simply the Best says the sign outside.
And it's true. Our suits are the best.
Mum makes them herself and I help
by cutting out the cloth. Famous
people often buy our suits.

That's why the famous Bellow came
to us.

'I want a special suit,' he said. 'I am singing at the Grand Opera House tomorrow night. Everyone will be coming.'

'We won't,' I said. 'We haven't got tickets.'

The great singer looked down his nose at me. 'As I was saying, a special suit. Something new. When I walk on stage I want everyone to look at me.'

'We will find you the best suit in the shop,' said Mum. 'I'm a big fan of yours, Mr Bellow.'

She started to measure him. He was so big we needed two tape measures. I had to stand on a chair and hold them round his chest. Rolo jumped up and down barking.

'Get that mutt away from me! I hate dogs!' shouted the great singer.

'He's not a mutt, he's Rolo,' I said. 'He only wants to join in the game.'

Rolo jumped up again. Bellow aimed a kick at him. He missed and kicked the chair.

'Ow! Get that dog out of here!' he roared.

Mum made me take Rolo into the
back of the shop. I could hear him
making little growling noises. He didn't
like the famous Bellow. Neither did I.

First, the great singer tried on a
brown check suit. He stood sideways
and looked in the mirror.

'No, too tight.'

Next, he tried a grey suit.

'Too dull, too boring.'

He tried one with a short black jacket.

'No, no, no! It makes me look like
a penguin.'

He tried a suit in bright red and
yellow stripes.

'What! You want me to look like a
circus tent?'

Mr Bellow tried on every suit in the shop. But nothing could please him. His face grew redder and redder. He stamped up and down, waving his hands in the air.

'This is too bad. I must have a new suit for the concert. Something new. I want everyone to look at me.'

Mum said, 'But Mr Bellow, you've tried every suit in the shop.'

'Then you must make me a new one.'

'But the concert is tomorrow! There isn't time!'

'I don't care if it takes you all night,' said the great singer. 'I'll come back for the suit in the morning. And I expect it to be ready.'

'What if it isn't?' I asked.

'Then I'll make sure no one buys a suit from you ever again!'

With that, the famous Bellow left, slamming the door. Rolo came out to bark after him as he marched down the street.

Mum sighed. 'He does have a voice like an angel.'

'Yes,' I said. 'And manners like a pig.'

2

That evening, Mum had her sewing machine out on the table. I made our dinner in the kitchen.

'It's no good,' she said. 'I can't think of anything that's really new.'

I put three bowls on the table. One for me, one for Mum, and one for Rolo.

'Never mind, Mum. Have some dinner. I've made spaghetti.'

Rolo wagged his tail. Spaghetti is his favourite. But Mum was too worried to eat. 'We've got to think of a suit for Mr Bellow,' she said.

'I don't see why. He's rude and he tried to kick Rolo,' I grumbled.

'But if we don't, he'll tell everyone not to buy our suits. We will have to close the shop.'

I didn't want that to happen. What would we do without the shop?

I played with the spaghetti, trying to think. As I wound it round my fork, the spaghetti got more and more tangled. It looked just like a ball of wool.

Then I had my idea.

'Mum, why don't we make him a suit from spaghetti?'

'Pardon?'

'Think about it,' I said. 'It would be new. No one has ever worn a suit made from spaghetti. And people would be amazed when he walked on stage.'

'It would make them stop and stare all right,' laughed Mum.

'And that's what he wants – everyone to look at him.'

'But can it be done?' asked Mum. 'Can a suit be made from spaghetti?'

There was only one way to find out. First we collected all the spaghetti in the house.

Then I boiled it in a big pan. We spread it out on the table to cool down. Rolo helped by eating any bits that fell on the floor.

When it was ready, Mum set to work. She is the best tailor in town. If anyone could make a spaghetti suit it was my Mum.

The two of us worked all night. In
the morning we opened the shop. The
famous Bellow was waiting outside.

'Well?' he said. 'Is my suit ready?
Is it something new?'

'It is,' smiled Mum. 'No one has
ever worn a suit like this.'

'Let's see it then. I want to try it
on,' said the great singer.

Mum nodded and I brought in the suit. It was white and it shone. The spaghetti was woven in amazing patterns.

Bellow's eyes nearly popped out of his head. 'What is it? I've never seen anything like it.'

'It's made from spaghetti,' I told him.

'Spaghetti? You don't say!'

'We do,' said Mum. 'But you must be very careful with it. If just one piece comes loose, the whole suit may come apart. Spaghetti is like that.'

The famous Bellow grabbed the suit.

'Tonight everyone will look at me. No one will forget the famous Bellow,' he said.

3

Mum and I had front seats for the concert that night. Mum paid for the tickets. She used the money Bellow paid us for the suit. Rolo came too of course. But I kept him under my coat. I didn't even tell Mum. Dogs aren't allowed in the Grand Opera House.

The musicians were tuning up. There
was a buzz of excitement. Everyone
had come to hear the famous Bellow
sing. The lights went down. Bellow
walked on stage. He bowed low.
Everyone gasped in amazement.

'Look at that suit!'

'How unusual!'

'The way it shines.'

'Those amazing patterns!'

'What can it be made of?'

Mum and I looked at each other.
Only we knew the secret of the
spaghetti suit.

24

The famous Bellow heard the
whispers. He smiled. He opened his
mouth and started to sing.

His voice filled the Grand Opera
House.

'See what I mean,' said Mum.
'A voice like an angel.'

The concert went well. At the end
everyone stood to clap and cheer.
Some ladies threw red roses onto the
stage. The famous Bellow bowed low.
He bent to pick up the roses. That was
when I noticed his trousers. A piece of
spaghetti had come loose.

I tried to tell him. I waved and pointed. But he didn't take any notice. He was too busy bowing and kissing his hands.

Then, as I was waving, Rolo jumped out from my coat. He was tired of keeping still for so long. And he'd seen the piece of spaghetti. It was dangling from the bottom of Bellow's trouser leg. Spaghetti was Rolo's favourite.

Before I could stop him, Rolo jumped
onto the stage. The famous Bellow
stepped back in alarm. He was scared
of dogs.

'Shoo! Go away, horrible little mutt!'
Rolo growled. He hadn't forgotten
how Bellow had tried to kick him. All
of a sudden he pounced on the loose
piece of spaghetti. He took it in his
teeth and pulled.

'Let go! Let go!' yelled the great
singer.

Rolo didn't let go. The piece of
spaghetti in his mouth grew longer
and longer. At the same time, Bellow's
trousers got shorter and shorter.

People started to point and giggle.
But Rolo didn't stop until he had
gulped down all the trousers. Even
the buttons.

The great singer was left in his underpants. He went very red and tried to hide himself behind the curtains. Now Rolo had his eye on the spaghetti jacket. He came after it, growling.

The famous Bellow gave a howl and fled from the stage. Rolo ran after Bellow. We ran after Rolo and a huge crowd ran after us, yelling and waving.

Out on the street, Rolo met some
friends. They all chased the great singer
down the road, snapping at what was
left of the jacket. People cheered as the
great Bellow scampered past in nothing
but his vest and pants and a few bits of
spaghetti.

'Well,' I said to Mum, 'he got what he
wanted. Everyone IS looking at him now.'

About the author

I have been writing stories for
radio, television and books
for many years. I live in
Nottingham and work in a
top attic room where no one
can disturb me. I often try
out my stories on my two
children at bath time. If
they stop shouting and
splashing me, I know it must be a good
story. *The Great Spaghetti Suit* started with
just a title. I got the idea of a spaghetti
suit and then just had to find someone
who might be daft enough to wear it.